waves $3:34

waves $1.99

Learn to Draw
INSECTS

www.av2books.com

AV² provides enriched content that supplements and complements this book. Weigl's AV² books strive to create inspired learning and engage young minds in a total learning experience.

Your AV² Media Enhanced books come alive with...

Audio
Listen to sections of the book read aloud.

Key Words
Study vocabulary, and complete a matching word activity.

Video
Watch informative video clips.

Quizzes
Test your knowledge.

Embedded Weblinks
Gain additional information for research.

Slide Show
View images and captions, and prepare a presentation.

Try This!
Complete activities and hands-on experiments.

... and much, much more!

Go to **www.av2books.com**, and enter this book's unique code.

BOOK CODE

J333349

AV² by Weigl brings you media enhanced books that support active learning.

Published by AV² by Weigl
350 5th Avenue, 59th Floor
New York, NY 10118
Website: www.weigl.com   www.av2books.com

Library of Congress Cataloging-in-Publication Data

Insects / edited by Heather Kissock.
    pages cm -- (Learn to draw)
ISBN 978-1-61913-241-2 (hardcover : alk. paper) -- ISBN 978-1-61913-246-7
(softcover : alk. paper)
1. Insects in art--Juvenile literature. 2. Drawing--Technique--Juvenile
literature. I. Kissock, Heather.
NC783.I57 2012
743.6'57--dc23
                        2012000465

Printed in the United States of America in North Mankato, Minnesota
1 2 3 4 5 6 7 8 9 0 16 15 14 13 12

042012
WEP050412

Senior Editor: Heather Kissock
Art Director: Terry Paulhus

Every reasonable effort has been made to trace ownership and to obtain permission to reprint copyright material. The publishers would be pleased to have any errors or omissions brought to their attention so that they may be corrected in subsequent printings.

Weigl acknowledges Getty Images as its primary image supplier for this title.

38888000173348

Contents

6

10

14

18

22

26

3

Why Draw?

Drawing is easier than you think. Look around you. The world is made of shapes and lines. By combining simple shapes and lines, anything can be drawn. An orange is just a circle with a few details added. A flower can be a circle with ovals drawn around it. An ice cream cone can be a triangle topped with a circle. Most anything, no matter how complicated, can be broken down into simple shapes.

circle

oval

circle → circle

circle →

triangle →

Drawing helps people make sense of the world. It is a way to reduce an object to its simplest form, say our most personal feelings and thoughts, or show others objects from our **imagination**. Drawing an object can help you learn how it fits together and works.

What shapes do you see in this car?

It is fun to put the world onto a page, but it is also a good way to learn. Learning to draw even simple objects introduces the skills needed to fully express oneself visually. Drawing is an excellent form of **communication** and improves people's imagination.

Practice drawing your favorite insects in this book to learn the basic skills necessary to draw. You can use those skills to create your own drawings.

Insects

Insects live in all parts of the world. Some live in snowcapped mountains. Others live in dry desert heat. Some even live in fresh water. Insects have lived on Earth for millions of years. Today, there are more than one million known insect **species**.

All insects have several common features. These animals have a hard exoskeleton. This is a shell or protective covering. Insects have three main body parts. They have a head, a **thorax**, and an **abdomen**. Insects are invertebrates. This means they do not have a backbone.

Each insect species also has its own special features. These features help them to live in different parts of the world. Drawing the insects in this book is a great way to learn about the different parts and features that make these insects successful in their environment. As you draw each part of the insects in this book, consider how that part benefits the animal. Think about how the animal would survive without that feature.

Meet the Ant

Ants are found on all of the world's continents except Antarctica. There are at least 20,000 types of ant in the world. They range in length from 0.07 to 1 inch (2 to 25 millimeters) and can be brown, black, yellow, or red in color.

Ants are social insects. This means they live in large groups. Ants live in colonies with thousands of other ants. Colonies are made up of many rooms and tunnels under the ground. Most ants live in the soil. Some live in wood. Others live in holes made inside plants.

Brain
Ants have the largest brains of all insects. An ant brain has about 250,000 **brain cells**. A human brain, on the other hand, has 10 trillion brain cells.

Antennae
An ant has two antennae. These antennae are jointed. This means they are made up of sections and can move around. The antennae are an ant's main **sense organ**. They allow ants to smell, touch, taste, and hear.

Eyes
Like most adult insects, ants have **compound eyes**. This means they are made up of many **lenses**. The lenses help the ants see movement very well.

Stomach

An ant has two stomachs. One stomach holds food for the ant. The other holds food for the ant's family. An ant stores food in its stomach until it reaches its family. Then, it spits out the food for the other ants to eat.

Stingers

Ants have poison sacs or stingers at the end of their abdomen. They use these to protect themselves against **predators**.

How to Draw an Ant

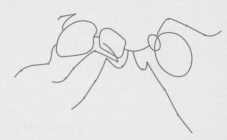

1 Start with a simple stick figure of the ant. Use ovals for the head and body, and lines for the legs and antennae. Now, join the ovals with a curved line, as shown.

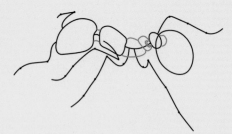

2 Draw the thorax of the ant.

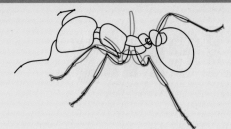

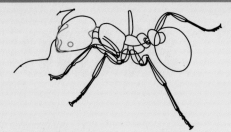

3 Next, draw the legs and claws.

4 In this step, draw the head and the eye.

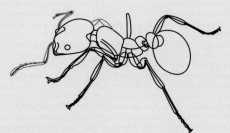

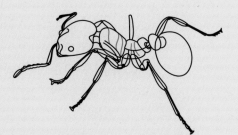

5 Next, draw the antennae and add one more leg.

6 Now, add details to the body.

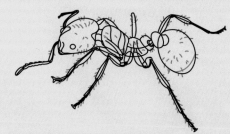

7 Draw hair on the body, antennae, and legs.

8 Erase the extra lines and the stick figure frame.

9 Color the image.

Meet the Butterfly

Butterflies are brightly colored insects with paper-thin wings. They can often be seen fluttering around flowers. Some butterflies have special markings that help them blend into the environment. This makes it difficult for predators to see them.

Butterflies range in size from 1.8 to 12 inches (4.5 to 30 centimeters). This is as small as a pin or as wide as a ruler. Butterflies weigh as little as two rose petals.

Antennae
A butterfly's head has two antennae. Butterflies use their antennae for balance and to smell objects.

Wings
Four delicate wings move the butterfly through the air. There are two wings in the front and two at the back. Butterflies can fly as fast as 30 miles (48 kilometers) per hour. When butterflies are resting, their wings stand up straight.

Thorax
A butterfly's thorax is separated into three parts. There is a pair of legs on each part. The thorax has muscles that help make the wings and legs move.

Mouth

A butterfly's mouth has a long tube that acts like a straw. This tube is called a proboscis. The proboscis is similar to a tongue. Butterflies uncoil it to sip nectar from inside flowers.

Eyes

Butterflies can see **ultraviolet rays**. Their eyes have many small lenses. These lenses capture light from the butterfly's range of view.

Legs

Each of a butterfly's six legs has sensors at its end. Butterflies use these sensors to taste food. The two front legs are sometimes shorter than the others. Butterflies use their front legs to clean their antennae.

How to Draw a Butterfly

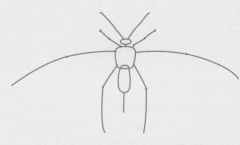

1 Start by drawing a stick figure of the butterfly. Use ovals for the head and body, and lines for the wings, antennae, abdomen, and legs.

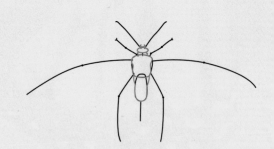

2 Now, draw the head, mouth, thorax, and abdomen.

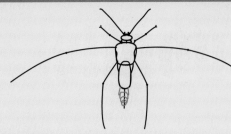 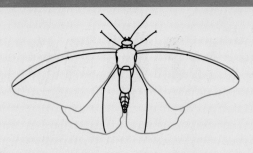

3 Next, complete the abdomen, as shown.

4 In this step, draw the wings.

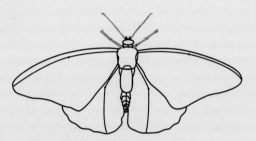 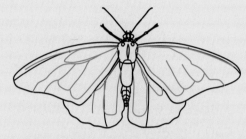

5 Next, draw the front legs and antennae.

6 Draw curved lines on the wings to make a pattern.

7 Draw more lines and circles to add detail to the pattern.

8 Erase the extra lines.

9 Color the image.

Meet the Dragonfly

A dragonfly is an insect with a long body and shiny wings. Dragonflies can often be seen zipping through the air. The dragonfly is the fastest insect on Earth. It flies at speeds of 30 to 60 miles (48 to 97 km) per hour.

Dragonflies live all over the world. They can live any place that has water nearby. Ponds, rivers, lakes, streams, and swamps are perfect places for dragonflies to live. In fact, most of a dragonfly's life is spent in water.

Legs
Dragonflies use their legs to catch **prey** in mid-air. To do this, the dragonfly forms its legs into a basket shape. The basket acts as a net to trap flies.

Wings
A dragonfly's wings often look like lace or glass. Dragonflies use their wings to fly forward, backward, upward, downward, and to turn. Unlike other flying insects, dragonflies can even use their wings to hover. This means that they can flap their wings to hold still in the air.

Jaws

A dragonfly has large jaws that contain several sharp teeth. The dragonfly sometimes uses its jaws to catch small insects.

Eyes

Dragonflies have the largest eyes of any insect. They have two huge eyes that cover most of their head. Each eye has up to 30,000 lenses. This helps a dragonfly to see even the smallest movement.

Abdomen

A dragonfly's abdomen is long and slim. It is made up of 10 parts. A dragonfly breathes through tiny holes in its abdomen and thorax.

How to Draw a
Dragonfly

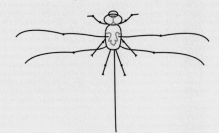

1 Make a stick figure frame of the dragonfly. Draw ovals for the head, jaws, and body, and lines for the legs, wings, and abdomen.

2 Draw the eyes and body details.

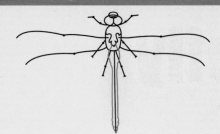
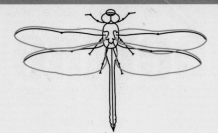
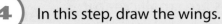

3 Next, draw the abdomen.

4 In this step, draw the wings.

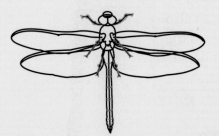
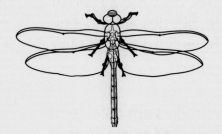

5 Now, draw the legs and segments on the abdomen.

6 Draw the claws and the patches on the thorax and abdomen.

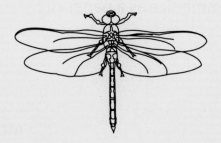

7 Draw lines on the wings, as shown.

8 Erase the extra lines and the stick figure frame.

9 Color the image.

Meet the Firefly

Fireflies are small creatures that light up the night during the summer months. They are a type of beetle. Beetles are insects that have hard covers over their wings.

Most fireflies are black and have two red spots on their head. Their outside shell is lined with yellow. Fireflies measure up to 1 inch (2.5 cm) long. This is the same size as a paper clip.

Antennae
A firefly's antennae act as feelers. They help the firefly find food. The antennae can also sense vibrations in the air that could mean a predator is near.

Mouth
Fireflies use their mouth to catch prey. They grasp at food using their jaws. Adult fireflies sometimes eat plant **pollen** and insects. Some fireflies do not eat at all.

Wings

Fireflies are the only glowing insects that have wings. Two tough outer wings protect the softer underwings and the body. Fireflies use their outer wings for balance during flight. The underwings are used to fly.

Abdomen

At night, the abdomen of the firefly can be seen glowing a bright yellow-green color. Fireflies flash their lights on and off to attract other fireflies. Their glow can barely be seen in daylight.

How to Draw a Firefly

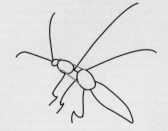

1 Draw a stick figure of the firefly. Use ovals for the body and head, and lines for the wings, antennae, and legs.

2 Now, join the body ovals with curved lines.

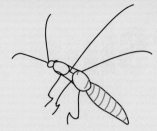
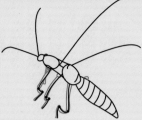

 3 Next, draw the segments on the abdomen.

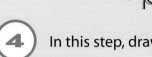 **4** In this step, draw the legs.

 5 Next, draw the eyes, mouth, and claws.

6 Now, draw the wings and antennae.

7 Draw curved lines on the wings and abdomen as shown.

8 Erase the extra lines and the stick figure frame.

 9 Color the image.

21

Meet the Grasshopper

The grasshopper is best known for its jumping ability. Grasshoppers are often seen hopping through grass and over roads. A grasshopper can leap up to 20 times the length of its own body.

Grasshoppers live in warm places all over the world. They are usually found among small plants that grow near the ground. Some also live near swamps. Most grasshoppers prefer dry places that have plenty of grass.

Eyes
A grasshopper has five eyes. Grasshoppers see through the two large eyes on either side of their head. Three smaller eyes measure changes in light.

Front Legs
A grasshopper uses its short front legs to hold food and to walk.

Jaws
A grasshopper's jaws are very strong. They are used for chewing food. Grasshoppers are herbivores. This means they only eat plants.

Wings

A grasshopper has two pairs of wings. The front wings act as hard covers for the hind wings. The hind wings are used to fly. Some grasshoppers rub their wings together to make music. Others rub their back legs across their front wings. This makes a chirping sound.

Ears

Grasshoppers do not have ears. They use organs called tympanums to pick up sounds. The tympanums are found in the grasshopper's abdomen.

Back Legs

Grasshoppers have muscular back legs. They use these long back legs for hopping.

How to Draw a Grasshopper

1. Start with a simple stick figure of the grasshopper. Use ovals for the head and body, and lines for the legs and antennae.

2. Now, draw the wings.

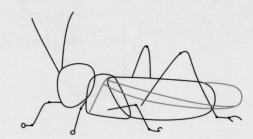

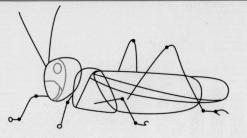

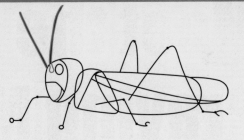

3 Draw the eye and jaws.

4 In this step, draw the antennae.

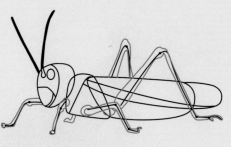

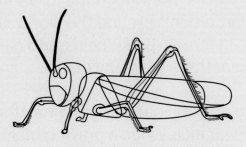

5 Next, draw the legs of the grasshopper.

6 Now, draw the spines on the legs.

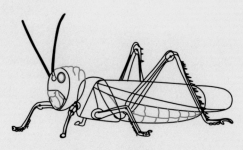

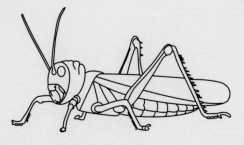

7 Draw the details on the head and abdomen.

8 Erase the extra lines.

9 Color the image.

Meet the Praying Mantis

Praying mantises have lived on Earth for more than 87 million years. They are found in warm environments around the world. They live in forests, parks, fields, and gardens where there are many plants.

The praying mantis was named for its appearance. When a praying mantis folds its legs toward its body, it looks like it is praying.

Head
The praying mantis is the only insect that can turn its head from side to side.

Color and Shape

To most people, praying mantises look like twigs or leaves. This is because they are the same color and shape as the plants they live on. Their shape and color act as a **camouflage**. They help praying mantises hide from predators and prey.

Wings

A praying mantis has two sets of wings. Praying mantises use their wings to scare away predators, such as birds. They fan their brightly colored wings when they see a predator. This makes the mantis look much larger than it is.

Legs

A praying mantis's front legs are used for grabbing and holding prey. Its other legs are used for walking, climbing, and jumping.

How to Draw a
Praying Mantis

1. Start with a stick figure of the praying mantis. Use ovals for the head and body, and lines for the legs.

2. Now, join the ovals with two lines, as shown.

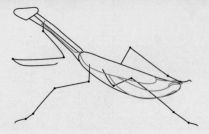

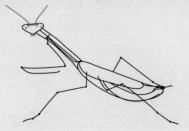

3 Draw the thorax and wings.

4 In this step, draw the eyes, mouth, and antennae.

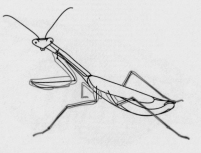

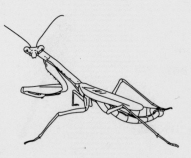

5 Next, draw the legs.

6 Draw the abdomen. Also draw spines on the legs.

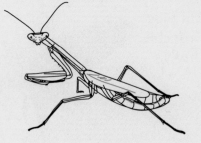

7 Add details to the wings and head.

8 Erase the extra lines and the stick figure frame.

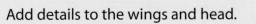

9 Color the image.

Test Your Knowledge of Insects

1. What kind of group does an ant live in?

Answer: A colony

2. What body part does a butterfly use to sip nectar?

Answer: Its proboscis

3. How is a dragonfly different from other flying insects?

Answer: It can use its wings to hover.

4. What type of insect is a firefly?

Answer: A beetle

5. How does a grasshopper hear?

Answer: It uses organs called tympanums to hear.

6. What is unique about the praying mantis?

Answer: It is the only insect that can turn its head from side to side.

Draw an Environment

Materials

- Large white poster board
- Internet connection or library
- Pencils and crayons or markers
- Glue or tape

Steps

1. Complete one of the insect drawings in this book. Cut out the drawing.
2. Using this book, the internet, and a library, find out about your insect and the environment in which it lives.
3. Think about what the insect might see and hear in its environment. What does its environment look like? What sorts of trees are there? Is there water? What does the landscape look like? Are there other animals in its environment? What in the insect's environment is essential to its survival? What other important features might you find in the insect's environment?
4. On the large white poster board, draw an environment for your insect. Be sure to place all the features you noted in step 3.
5. Place the cutout insect in its environment with glue or tape. Color the insect's environment to complete the activity.

Glossary

abdomen: part of the body where the digestive organs are found

brain cells: nerve cells in the brain. A cell is the basic structural unit of all organisms.

camouflage: a device used for concealment

communicaton: the sending and receiving of information

compound eyes: eyes that are made up of many small visual units

imagination: the ability to form new creative ideas or images

lenses: parts of the eyes that focus images

pollen: a fine powder produced by plants

predators: animals that hunt other animals for food

prey: animals that are hunted by other animals for food

sense organ: a structure in animals that receives information and sends it to the brain

species: type or sort

thorax: the part of the body where legs and wings are attached

ultraviolet rays: rays of light that are invisible to the human eye

Log on to www.av2books.com

AV² by Weigl brings you media enhanced books that support active learning. Go to www.av2books.com, and enter the special code found on page 2 of this book. You will gain access to enriched and enhanced content that supplements and complements this book. Content includes video, audio, weblinks, quizzes, a slide show, and activities.

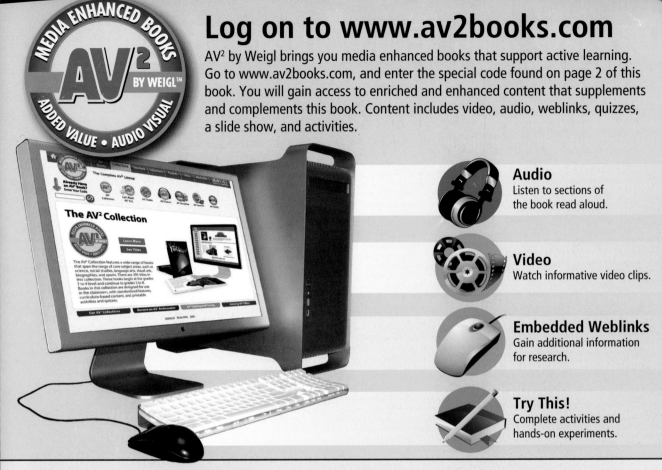

Audio
Listen to sections of the book read aloud.

Video
Watch informative video clips.

Embedded Weblinks
Gain additional information for research.

Try This!
Complete activities and hands-on experiments.

WHAT'S ONLINE?

Try This!	Embedded Weblinks	Video	EXTRA FEATURES
Complete an interactive drawing tutorial for each of the six insects in the book.	Learn more about each of the six insects in the book.	Watch a video about insects.	**Audio** Listen to sections of the book read aloud.
			Key Words Study vocabulary, and complete a matching word activity.
			Slide Show View images and captions, and prepare a presentation.
			Quizzes Test your knowledge.

AV² was built to bridge the gap between print and digital. We encourage you to tell us what you like and what you want to see in the future.

Sign up to be an AV² Ambassador at www.av2books.com/ambassador.